ANGELS IN
Suits

KARREN HILL GORDON

ANGELS IN SUITS

Karren Hill Gordon

Edited by Willie Mae Jackson

Designed by Kristen Marie Feaster

ANGELS IN SUITS

Reflection | Tribute | Call to Action

As Hill Gordon reflects back on her personal and professional journey, she pays tribute to a special group of people who were instrumental in her development and success. Subsequently, she encourages women to use some of the same resources and strategies she describes in *Angels in Suits*. She calls for action to help women progress in leadership roles. Through her collection of experiences and fond memories, she highlights the positive ways fathers, pastors, husbands, mentors, and friends can contribute to the development of confident and effective women leaders.

Karren Hill Gordon is a professional consultant, mentor, and community leader. She has a special interest in leadership development for teen girls and young women.

Trafford rev. 01/25/2022

 www.trafford.com
North America & international
toll-free: 844-688-6899 (USA & Canada)
fax: 812 355 4082

This book is dedicated to my daughter, Kristen. I hope that you will be inspired by the contents of this project. It is my prayer that you will have the vision to always see the angels placed in your life. Remember to always be appreciative to those surrounding you with hope, encouragement, and support.

This project is also dedicated to my stepdaughter, Brittany and my nieces, Antilla and Jameela. I hope that you will find something that I have shared useful as you grow into strong and confident young women.

Acknowledgements

I want to express my deepest thanks to my husband, friend, confidant, critic and number one supporter. I am indebted to him for his constant love and loyalty. *Chris, I love you dearly!*

I wish to thank my father, Anthriest Hill, Sr., for his unwavering encouragement. I will always remember his support with all of my endeavors from childhood to adulthood. Daddy, thanks for being a motivator!

A big hug and kiss goes to my brother, Anthriest Hill, Jr., for his help over the years while Chris was overseas. I appreciate his willingness to stand in the gap. *Thank you brother dear!*

Finally, I must acknowledge two influential women in my life. My mother, Frances Dicks Hill, is a very strong, caring and confident woman. She was my father's true partner in my rearing. In addition, I have been blessed to have a treasured lifelong relationship with my big sister, Angela Hill Harmon. I have learned much from them and I have valued their support. *I love you both very much. Stay forever strong!*

Introduction

Chapter 1: In the Beginning: A Father's Influence

Chapter 2: Campus Corner: Male Dominance

Chapter 3: A Man of Grace: My Pastor

Chapter 4: Fallen: My Soul Mate

Chapter 5: The World of Work: From East to West

Chapter 6: Coaching on the Sidelines

Chapter 7: Special Edition: Suit Without a Tie

Chapter 8: The Quest: What Can I Do?

Chapter 9: A Call to Action: What Can Women Do?

Chapter 10: Leap into Leadership

Chapter 11: Special Thanks to My
Brothers and Sisters

Introduction

This book is a tribute to an elite group of individuals and a call to action for others. I openly pay tribute to several people who have been instrumental in my development and pursuit to excel. Yet, I also want to make an appeal to others. My appeal is simple. I ask that women begin to make special efforts to network and support each other. As we come together as a collective body to share experiences, cultivate relationships and utilize resources, we create a powerful equation.

On more than one occasion, I have been inspired to document the positive impact of several people in my life. Initially, I was moved by the willing spirit and selfless acts of these particular people to help me on my journey. Later, I was moved by an increased level of frustration resulting from the lack of support and camaraderie among many women I have encountered while on this path. On so many occasions, I witnessed a variety of male bashing sessions, and I felt it would be meaningful to share my story. It is my desire to spark a light of hope among other women and serve as a source of motivation. For these reasons, I decided to share excerpts of my brief and simple journey.

I wanted to pay tribute to this elite group of men because it was their actions and support that cracked open doors of opportunity for me. Some prayed and some shared words of encouragement. Some took the time to provide specific consultation while others simply shared a lunch hour to give advice. I know that God strategically placed these special people in my life and I am very grateful.

Many months after I began this project, I had an interesting encounter with a friend. I briefly shared the purpose of what I was writing and why I was writing about it. Then,

I inquired about references to angels in the Bible. He said that he would send me some information via email. However, before we ended the telephone conversation he shared some interesting comments. He said, "When angels appeared in human society, they resembled normal males and never came dressed as women. In whatever form they occurred, however, their general purpose was to declare and promote God's will." He was reading from a Bible Study tool web site. I don't profess to be a biblical scholar nor do I plan to focus on those statements. However, I decided to mentally digest what I heard. Subsequently, I claimed those statements as affirmations to the value of my project. I was encouraged to continue to write about my experiences and the guardian angels I encountered during my brief journey here on earth. I am grateful to my friend, Reverend Ellis White, Jr. for sharing it with me.

As I continued to reflect back on my life and analyze the wonderful people I have encountered and the many blessing I have received, I marvel at the goodness of God. I am even more excited about the possibilities and the opportunities that the future holds. As I think about the special people and their acts of kindness, I am reminded of the many examples in the Bible of the roles and purpose of angels. The following words come to mind: guide, protect, strengthen, encourage, and deliver. Although there are many passages in the Bible demonstrating angels in such roles, I can immediately give thanks for my *angels in suits* that take such actions everyday. Not long ago, a colleague was visiting my office and we were discussing the volatile times with the job market, economy and the turmoil of our international status. As he was leaving my office, he said, "I don't know who's looking out for you, but he's doing a good job." I simply smiled as I lifted my eyes upward and said, "You are absolutely right. I am truly blessed."

Although it is important for me to recognize these special men, it becomes more important for me to work harder to share with other women and encourage the building of a strong support system for my sisters. I am committed to making a difference and I hope that the contents of these pages will encourage others to explore ways to change their thinking and behaviors. Recognizing that it is all right to be competitive, assertive and resourceful, I truly hope that more women will band together and support each other. Together we can encourage, support, congratulate and applaud each other.

I hope that through my sharing, others will be inclined to strive to build better bridges and networks, particularly among women. This is not to imply that I have not had valued relationships and support of other women. Nor does it imply that I have not encouraged or given support to other women. My sharing is designed to depict how fragmented those influences have been and to simply illustrate how I have been able to achieve professional and personal goals with the tremendous support of males both family and friends. I know that it was nothing special about me but all about the special qualities and abilities of my guardian angels. They have positively impacted my life and the lives of so many others. For that favor, I am forever grateful.

I recognize that many opportunities and a great deal of guidance have come as a result of several good folks who happened to be men. I often reflect back on the many episodes of guidance and advice given to me. I say thank you my angels in suits. However, I am more focused on my role in influencing the ways in which women can network, advise, and assist other women. I certainly want to share my guardian angels with them, but I want to engage in a more primary role helping women achieve and pursue their dreams.

Today, I am committed to helping other sisters when I can. I hope that I will be able to make a difference through the establishment of the Support Your Sister (SYS) Network. After long hours of thought and prayer, I was guided to create a venue for young women to come together to share, learn, and support each other. I have come to learn that several members have male mentors and advisors. Many have expressed similar concerns and experiences regarding obstacles with female supervisors and colleagues. Thus, there is a great need to give attention to this matter. It would behoove us to review and monitor research on this issue and participate in developing solutions for camaraderie, mentoring, and leadership among women.

Furthermore, my role as a parent of a young impressionable girl, an aunt and model to other young girls in my church and community places an even greater weight on my heart to make a difference. Even if my contribution is just one of many ingredients or a simple piece to the big puzzle, I want to make a difference. This is my vision for succeeding in life. I believe that one cannot equate success and wealth only to dollar figures and material possessions. I believe that an accomplished individual may find success and wealth through the lives of those he or she has touched. Therefore, the ability to leave a positive mark while here on earth and make a difference is far greater than accumulating enormous amounts of cash. Consequently, I know that I must take my good fortune and bless others. I am obligated to take what I have learned and use it to help others along the journey. As I collect lessons learned from my distinct group of guardian angels, I am obligated to share with other women as well as encourage them to engage in such strategies and approaches in order to excel in their chosen endeavors.

For the past couple of years, I have been particularly interested in the plight of women as it relates to my own personal experiences. I wanted to get a clearer picture on the status of women in South Carolina. My involvement with various associations has been enlightening. Accessing information through the Leadership Institute at Columbia College and the American Association of University Women has affirmed my perceptions and motivated me to be a part of the solution. Many studies have been conducted in all parts of the country on various aspects of women in society. The data clearly reveals that women are still underrepresented in leadership roles in business, underpaid in comparable positions as their male counterparts, and underrepresented in elected capacities.

I became more discouraged after the release of a study on the status of women in South Carolina published by the Institute for Women's Policy Research in November 2002. South Carolina earned a grade of D. This statewide analysis examined employment earnings, political participation, health and well-being, reproductive rights, and the social and economic autonomy of women. What a blow! This simply confirmed that not only do women need to work together but we should also continue to build alliances with men who have already demonstrated their commitment to equal access and opportunity for women. We should work side by side with policy makers, community leaders and employers to improve conditions for women. Today, I challenge men and women to come together and produce better outcomes. It will help women move forward and take our rightful place in society. Contrary to popular belief, all men are not part of the Good-Old Boy Network. There are some real *angels in suits* out there that really make a difference.

On Fatherhood...
"It doesn't matter who my father was; it matters
who I remember he was."
-Anne Sexton

My father, Anthriest Hill, Sr.
Sumter, South Carolina 1990

Chapter 1

In the Beginning: A Father's Influence

Yᵒᵘ may ask what is so special about him. Why is his influence so significant? Well, he was born in 1938 in Muscogee County, Georgia. He grew up on a farm where he came to understand the value of family and hard work, and he was a young man with vision. He was determined to do better and excel. At the age of seventeen, he left home and joined the U.S. Army. No matter how difficult the training or task placed before him, he was fully motivated to beat all odds. He would say to himself that nothing would set him back and cause him to return to that farm. Whenever he became doubtful or weary, he reflected back on his childhood experiences at the farm and it gave him the inner strength to keep pushing forward. This is an individual who endured two tours in Vietnam that totaled 24 months of frontline combat in the war. Yet, he returned home without injury or scar. He was decorated with the Bronze Star Medal with the V Device and two Oak Leaf Clusters for heroism and leadership demonstrated while his unit was under intense fire. He endured international conflict and a home front battle of civil rights which set many limitations on the opportunities for black men during that time. He is a man of faith with an exceptional testimony. He retired Command Sergeant Major after serving twenty six years in the *army. Following this milestone, he worked an additional eighteen years with a private security firm and retired as a district manager in May 2000. This too was a challenging experience. There were various corporate hurdles he had to overcome. He met the challenge and excelled. The many lessons learned and successful strategies used would later become strong components of advice to me and many others. His collection of experiences shaped and molded him into the great man, husband and father that many will remember.*

As I look back over the challenges my father faced, I am amazed at his accomplishments and his constant motivation to reach one's full potential. He demanded that one never settle for anything in life. He attributes all of his success to hard work and the goodness of God. This young man from a small family farm somehow managed to successfully send his three children to college without government assistance or external financial obligation. He gave us a debt free head start in life and I am very grateful. It is evident why he has been so instrumental in my life. Let me share a brief excerpt of our journey together...

He stood tall and strong like a tree. He was as quiet as the spring winds swishing through the screens of the porch. He had the frame of a giant but the hug of a cuddly teddy bear. He commanded respect but easily earned affection. Even when he was away for extended periods of time while in the military, he managed to maintain my respect and affection from a distance.

I remember the talks in the car, at the foot of his bed, under the carport, and on the telephone. He was always interested in what was going on in my life, and he always had a bit of advice for me. This came at times even when I didn't want to hear it. Topics ranged from class work, boys, money, family and the future. From middle school crushes to high school saga, to college drama and then to adulthood, my father always had words to share about males. He always demonstrated how a man could support and uplift a woman with class, grace and affection. There were times he would simply make me want to scream because I really didn't agree with his direction. Yet, I knew deep inside that he was right and he was concerned. I knew that he only wanted the best for me and wanted me to want the best for myself.

I distinctly remember the times during my childhood when he would take me to his office to spend time with him. I got the chance to see my dad in action. He commanded respect and spoke with authority. He was tough but caring for the individuals under his supervision. My dad also had a strong presence in my life at home. There were instances when he would stay home with me to care for me when I was sick. He always had time for me and he always encouraged me. Daddy would always say, "You can do anything you want to do". That comment developed into long conversations over the years. My father always prodded me to explore my options, set high standards and always do my best. He often reminded me that consistency and patience were keys to accomplishing goals. We often laugh and joke about the days of the past. He gets a kick out of teasing me about things I did as a child. He has saved letters, photos and other memorabilia over the years. I know that I have always been important to him. I realize that he has made sacrifices and sent up many prayers on my behalf. His unconditional love and support have positively impacted my life. He continues to inspire me to aim high and reach for my dreams. He continues to be a centering force in my life and he helps me through difficult times and challenges.

Although we all have busy and complicated lifestyles, I still find comfort and contentment by his side on Sunday afternoons. We watch old movies, roast peanuts and talk. We routinely discuss matters of faith, education, politics and economic affairs. He is a great father and one of my guardian angels. It is unfortunate that every little girl does not have the opportunity to grow up safe with a loving and caring father. It is disheartening to know that every little girl is not afforded the opportunity to observe the grace of a gentle giant from childhood to adulthood. It is with overwhelming sadness that I reflect back on the shattered lives of so many of my former young clients who were victims of so many injustices rendered to them by their own fathers.

Yet, I share my own experience to acknowledge my father and other fathers who truly protected and uplifted their daughters. I also share this experience to strike a sense of hope for young women who are mothers or will become mothers because fathers can have a tremendous impact on the lives of their daughters. Their positive influence can have life-long effects and it may help shape strong and confident women. I thank God everyday for my angel, Anthriest Hill, Sr.

4-5-90

Hello Dad's Girl:

Just a short note; here are some pictures and other things Mom is sending to you. We enjoyed talking with you last night and I hope that you will continue to take care of yourself. We are looking forward to the arrival of the new stinker. Mom and I miss the other three already. (Smile) There's not very much to say because we are talking with you each week. Just remember Mom and I love both of you very much, (You and Chris) So, take care, will talk to you soon.

Love, Dad

(This is the only letter I have from my father.)

My father in Long Ann Province, South Vietnam, 1967.

> On Education...
> "Education is not a form of entertainment, but a means of empowering people to take control of their lives."
> -Unknown

Chapter 2

Campus Corner: Male Dominance

1982-1985
College of Criminal Justice
University of South Carolina
Columbia, South Carolina

President .... Male
College Dean .... Male
Academic Advisor .... Male
Professors .... Predominantly Males

Familiar Names:
Holderman
Mathias
Barrineau
Matthews
Chisolm
Montgomery
Gray

During this brief chapter of my life, I encountered an overwhelming presence of men in powerful and leadership positions on campus and in the criminal justice field. Although I did not cultivate any strong relationship with any particular individual, my reflection upon my college years are overshadowed by a strong male presence and a lack of connection to female faculty or student body support. However, I must acknowledge that the campus experience was rich and beneficial. I learned a great deal in the program and developed marketable skills during my internship as well as my part-time job in the Dean's Office. Yet, I longed for informal and formal support networks as a developing young woman preparing for a career path while I was discovering the many wonders of the world.

Today, as I reflect back on that experience, I am motivated to engage in the lives of young women attending college. My response to this gap in my life is to fill this void for someone else. Fortunately, I have been embraced by the faculty at Columbia College and I have been afforded the opportunity to participate in a pilot mentoring project for their students. As a part of the Leader2leader Mentoring Project, I was paired with Shanitra Singleton. It has been a very rewarding experience. Although my life seems to be filled with many activities, I take pride in making the time to be a part of Shanitra's journey. I don't take this role lightly and I try to make sure that our time spent together has worth. Yes, I like the fact that we get along and that we are from the same hometown. However, I think it is important that we spend time discussing important issues and seeking opportunities for growth and development. In addition to spending time getting to know each other, we have very focused discussions on specific topics. We have spent time addressing our different roles, leadership, time management, public speaking, risk taking, decision making and future projects. Shanitra has an interest in developing an effective mentoring project for middle school girls. So as I venture into a similar project with the local branch of the American Association of University Women, I will be sharing with her any helpful information I discover. Also, I plan to invite her to assist with our project in order to provide some hands on experience as well as give her an opportunity to explore the educational system to aide in the development of her project. Exposure to school district personnel, policies, volunteer programs and other sources should be a good starting point for her.

We are now in our second academic term for the Leader2leader project. I was pleased to know that Shanitra wanted to continue our mentoring relationship, and she did not want to be paired with a different person for her sophomore year. I hope that this experience has been beneficial to her because it has definitely been a positive and rewarding time for me. In the future, I hope to remain connected in some way to young women in college and provide some degree of support and encouragement.

On Christianity...
Let your light shine before men, that they may see
your good works, and glorify your Father which is in
heaven.
-Matthew 5:16

The Late Reverend Otis J. Nelson, Sr.
Sunrise: March 23, 1917
Sunset: January 31, 2003

Chapter 3

A Man of Grace: My Pastor

*T*his gentleman was born in Ridgeway, South Carolina and raised in Dabbs Crossroads and Goodwill Presbyterian Church. He attended Goodwill Parochial School in Sumter County through the eighth grade. Then he attended Brainard Institute in Chester County. He furthered his education at Johnson C. Smith University in North Carolina and South Carolina State University in Orangeburg where he earned a bachelor's degree in Agriculture. He was an educator and later became the principal of the former Johnson High School in Sumter District Two. During his teaching profession, he was rooted in a Methodist community so he eventually joined the Methodist church. He recalls his father as the major source of motivation to him. His father, the late Warren Julius Nelson was a Presbyterian minister for forty-one years. He later followed in his father's foot steps and joined the ranks in ministry and became licensed to preach in 1951. He was ordained as a Deacon in October 1953 and ordained as an Elder in 1954. He became fully connected with the United Methodist Church in 1954. As a minister and educator, his generosity and openness allowed him to reach long and wide throughout his community to help many people. He has been a guardian angel to many men and women over the years. I have witnessed others share their stories

13

in formal and informal settings about his kindness and helpfulness.
Let me share a little of my story about his specific role in my growth
and development…

I grew up in a very small church in which the majority of the membership was related in some form or fashion. My maternal grandmother and maternal grandfather had roots in this church. I have a rich family history there and I am still uncovering family treasures to pass on to my children.

As I look back on days passed, I remember special events such as vacation bible school, Sunday school and youth fellowship activities. I can remember a long list of pastors and their family members. Yet, there is one particular pastor that stands out in my mind. He too was a guardian angel placed in my life. I met him during a very crucial time in my life. I was a young adult. My desire to remain actively involved with the church was beginning to fade.

When I was a child, I was so carefree. When I became a youth, the church was a foundation for me to help me stay focused to deal with challenges and grow in the faith. However, as a young adult, I had a reality check. I was faced with the new world of work and began interacting with so many different types of people. It was a real change. To add to the confusion, I found myself witnessing similar dilemmas among the adults at my church. Politics, position and influence took on a different shade, but the dynamics were the same. Slowly, I began to lose interest and considered becoming disengaged. Then, along came a man who would have a life long impact on me.

Initially, I thought he was a man with whom I had absolutely nothing in common. He was not from my hometown and we were not related. He was retired and appeared to be an old man. I really didn't think he had the skill or influence to keep me engaged. He would have to show me something very powerful to keep my attention. That is exactly what he did!

He was an educated man and clung to two books ever so tightly. His favorite books were the Holy Bible and the Book of Discipline for the United Methodist Church. When there was confusion about anything, he always had a verse or text for reference to answer questions or provide guidance. He was remarkably encouraging. He was patient and very honest. Overtime, he won me over and managed to keep me involved in the church. He was instrumental in my pursuit of leadership roles and growing.

When Chris and I decided to get married, he was there for us. He secured a very special place in my heart. A couple of years later when my daughter was born in Austin, Texas, I came home for her baptism. He was aging and Kristen was a plump bundle of joy. So, I warned him not to drop her during the ceremony. (We had the kind of relationship that included humor and laughter.)

A few years later, we moved back to South Carolina where we purchased our first home. I certainly wanted it to be properly blessed. Although he was no longer the pastor of our church, he was still "my pastor" and he had to be a part of this special event. He agreed to participate in the ceremony. For over fifteen years into my adulthood, he remained supportive of all my endeavors. I will be forever grateful to him for his guidance, prodding and prayers. He pushed me to do more and stood by me every step of the way. When I became weak and shunned by human behaviors, he helped me to seek God's will and look beyond mortal shortcomings. He aided in the development of my desire for service to others.

On January 31, 2003, he slipped away into his eternal rest. When I learned of his passing, my heart was saddened and I wept. Later that morning, a friend told me that as time passes, my tears would turn into smiles and my time of grieving would turn into a time of reflection. Yes, the time of reflection is powerful, because I can slip back into a time of wonderful memories that will give me encouragement to continue to move forward in life and leave a good mark as he did.

Although he will be greatly missed, his legacy will live on in the lives of those he touched along the way. My husband reminded me that I must continue to make "Rev" proud. Surely, all that I have learned from him and all of the encouragement I received from him warrant a strong commitment to do something positive and powerful with my life.

Once again, I was in God's favor! Reverend Otis J. Nelson was another angel placed in my life to help me on my journey. His teaching and pushing made a real difference for me. His advocacy for education, perseverance and leadership has remained with me over the years. During our final visits together, it was uplifting for me to be in his presence. I often intended to drop by and cheer him up, but in his own quiet and subtle way, he made my heart glad.

Several months ago, I had an opportunity visit with him one afternoon at his home and share a portion of my draft manuscript with him. I wanted him to know how he impacted my life. Although I was unable to complete this project before his passing, he knew how special he was to me. I am very thankful that I had the opportunity to be in his presence and learn from him. *Reverend Nelson, your legacy will always live on through those you have touched along the way. I am so glad God sent you my way! You will be missed but I know that you are still watching over me.*

This poem was printed in the obituary for Reverend O.J. Nelson.It captures the essence of his personality and the life he lived

The Bridge Builder
-Author Unkown

An old man traveling a long highway,
Came at the evening cold and gray,
To a chasm vast deep and wide,
Through which was flowing a sullen tide.
The old man crossed in the twilight dim
To sullen stream held no fear for him;
But he turned when safe on the other side,
And build a bridge to span the tide.

"Old man," cried a fellow pilgrim near,"
Your journey will end with the closing day;
You never again will pass this way.
You have crossed the chasm deep and wide,
Why build this bridge at even-tide?"

The builder lifted his old gray head;
"Good friend, in the path I have come," He said
"There followeth after me today
A youth whose feet must pass this way.
This stream which has been a naught to me,
To that fair-haired youth may a pitfall be;
He too must cross the twilight dim-
Good friend, I build the bridge for him."

On Marriage...
In marriage, each partner is to be an encourager rather than a critic, forgiver rather than a collector of hurts, an enabler rather than a reformer."
-H. Norman Wright and Gary Joliver

My husband, Christopher T. Gordon
Shaw Air Force Base, South Carolina 2000

Chapter 4

Fallen: My Soul Mate

*H*e has stood the test of time. His journey has been full of storms and surprises. Yet, his faith, will power, and vision has allowed him to overcome many obstacles. He has taken the good from such experiences to motivate him and others. Surviving a parental abduction, abuse, poverty, foster care and rejection, he developed into an optimistic individual and strives daily to keep moving forward. His parents divorced when he was very young and he was the eldest of four children. Although he loved to read and had exceptional academic ability, fate did not avail a lot of guidance and support to pursue college and explore the options unfolding for young black men.

After graduating from high school, he enlisted into the US Air Force. There were peaks and valleys in his personal and professional journey. Taking advantage of training and educational opportunities while in the Air Force, he began to set a course for achievement and excellence. At the age of thirty seven, he retired from the Air Force and continued to pursue a career in information technology. Traditionally, this industry has been occupied by white males but he seems to welcome this challenge.

I have also admired him over the years for his self-discipline and his quest to excel. Chris constantly speaks of the life long jour-

21

ney of learning. He spends lots of time online ordering books, magazines and other resources. He consistently sets a pace to study and embarks upon achievement through levels of professional certifications. Being a supportive wife, I try to keep the house quiet and conducive for learning. So, I often leave him home alone and spend time at the mall and other sites of entertainment to help him out. This has been a long standing tradition in our house because whenever it was study time for promotions in the Air Force, I would make sure he had something to eat and then off to the mall I went. Believe it or not, he was always interested in what I picked up rather than annoyed about my spending. I was never inclined to sneak items in the house or leave them in the trunk as I have heard stories from other women. Let me briefly share portions of our journey together to illustrate the significance of his influence in my life...

It was a crisp evening in downtown Sumter on February 3, 1987. I was simply waiting at a traffic light to make a left turn and this handsome young man passed through the light. It happened within a matter of seconds. Our eyes met once and then he was gone. I circled the block for a parking space and went inside a small store to make a purchase. Minutes later as I approached the cashier, he came strolling in the front doors of the store. I knew it was all over for me. That was sixteen years ago. We fell in love, got married and created a family.

Instead of sharing stories of romance and marriage, I want to share a paradox with you. It is the part of my journey that is so different from many military spouses that I have met over the years. Although my husband's career was rooted in the Air Force, he always supported me in my efforts to achieve. Instead of relinquishing my rights and desires only to support his endeavors, we were always a team pushing forward together. I was always encouraged to pursue my individual goals. As we traveled and interacted with other military couples, we took pride in our effort to maintain focus in our partnership and pursuit of happiness for our family.

On January 16, 1988, we were married and remained in Sumter. Then in 1990, we moved to Austin, Texas and lived there for a couple of years. In 1992, we moved to Montgomery, Alabama as a result of Chris' assignment to Maxwell Air Force Base. Once again, I found myself in a city away from family and friends. It was a place filled with the unknown and the unfamiliar. After working a few months at a private non-profit organization, we knew that I wanted to do more and that I was capable of handling more responsibilities. Chris was always asking questions and looking for leads with his colleagues. With the hand of God working through many people, he utilized his newly established network to seek better options for me. He came home one evening with a job announcement, application and a map with directions to the office. I took it from there. As it worked out, I was offered the position. Even though Chris was dealing with own issues at the base, he was not only focused on himself. He was concerned about me and took the time to help. As my true partner and friend, he was there for me.

About six months later, we received orders to South Carolina. This was great! I was excited about going back home to be near my family. I was also pleased that I would have an opportunity to re-engage with the old network I had cultivated in previous years. However, I found myself unemployed and looking for work again. It was January 1994 and it was back to the drawing board. Chris would be departing to go to school in Mississippi for six months. He was cross-training into a very exciting and marketable field. He was about to enter into an intense educational journey. This would benefit him tremendously with his military career as well as stack the deck in his favor upon retirement. Yet, I found myself sitting around with mixed emotions. Another move forward for him and another job search for me.

A few days before his departure, Chris was reading the newspaper and came across a position announcement he thought I might be interested in pursuing. It was a Saturday night and the deadline for the application packet was Monday. The copy shops were closed in town that night and Chris suggested that we drive from Sumter to Columbia and work up the application packet at a Kinkos. I took him up on his offer.

After we completed the paperwork at Kinkos, he drove me to the post office to ensure proper postmark before midnight. By the time we returned to Sumter, it was about 1:00am on Sunday morning. We were approximately two miles from the house and we instantly became victims of a hit and run vehicle crash. By the grace of God, we were not seriously injured in the accident and we only required minimal medical attention. So much was happening so fast. We were dealing with the accident, relocating and preparing for a lengthy separation. He was scheduled to leave for Mississippi a couple of days later.

The day arrived for his departure. Yet, moments before he left, he looked at me and said, "If you are offered the position, try it for awhile and if you discover that you don't like it, you can always do something else." Chris managed to find a quick moment to reassure me that even though he would be far away, I had his support no matter how things turned out. In just a few words, he assured me that it was important to have a job that I enjoyed and it was okay to keep exploring other opportunities.

Chris finished school in September and we moved to Columbia. For a while things were going great. Then in the fall of 1996, we were faced with another difficult decision. He received orders to Italy. We were torn with staying together and living abroad for a while or dealing with an extensive separation. After conducting some research on the status of the base and assessing my career status, we agreed that it would not be to my advantage in the long run to move at that point. We made a difficult choice but a good choice. Chris went to Italy unaccompanied and that shortened his tour.

Once we made the decision for him to go alone, he began to encourage me to go to graduate school. We discussed our long-term plans and considered our options. Since Chris was five years away from retirement, it was important for us to really concentrate on my future career move. Therefore, after long discussions and preparation, I agreed to go back to school. The day before Chris left for Italy, he went with me to register for school. The next morning at the airport, I made a promise to him.

Christopher and I taking a
moment at the family reunion.
Atlanta, Georgia 2001

I assured him that I would have my degree when he completed his tour in Italy. I was committed because he was committed to me and my future. I knew that it was very likely that we would have to move again when he returned from Italy, and I knew it would be in my best interest to complete the program within two years. Otherwise, I would be faced with the complexities of school transfers and prolonged financing. It was difficult but I persevered.

On July 2, 1998, Chris completed his tour and came back to the United States. On July 22, 1998, I completed the final exam for my last class in the program. Fortunately, we did not have to relocate but it was wise to stick with my goal. It was a real challenge going to school, working full time and parenting alone. With the support of family and friends, I achieved my goal.

The following year, I took a little break from pacing my personal goals and became more involved with my daughter's school. Within in a matter of months, I became a volunteer, homeroom parent and member of the School Improvement Council. I also took great interest in the administration of the school and other community activities. After awhile, I found myself incorporating my interest in public school systems into long-term personal goals and began to set the pace.

A year later, I expressed to Chris my interest in entrepreneurial endeavors and immediately, he began to think of ways in which he could help me, well, help us succeed. So we began having planning sessions and the rest is history. We have a partnership! I can think of other acquaintances who shared with me that when they expressed their aspirations to start a business, they lacked spousal support. I recognize my blessing!

Chris has always supported and encouraged me. Often times, he would tell me not to come straight home from work every day. He knew there were organized groups I wanted to connect with at some point. Yet, I felt guilty and wanted to come home and prepare dinner and help out with homework. As the years passed, I began to let go of the superwoman syndrome and give my family more independence. I am still a little uncomfortable staying out late for business meetings and missing family time at the dinner table. Yet, I know that the family is fed and homework is done in my absence. We have a true partnership and we work as a team to benefit our family.

Even today, Chris continues to support me and express his interest in my career moves and personal growth. Shortly after he retired from the Air Force, he said something to me that was very touching. He looked at me and said, "If the opportunity comes, I will gladly move and follow you anywhere." This reaffirmed my husband's ability to see great things for us together. Again, I witnessed another selfless act. He recognized that I willingly moved several times due to his assignments, and he loves me enough to do the same for me. He values me not only as a wife but a skilled and talented individual with the potential to be a part of something great. We will only be successful if we support each other's endeavors. He has been a constant source of inspiration to me.

Thank you Chris! The encouragement, support, and criticism have been helpful over the years. I am forever grateful. We have just scratched the surface. The best is yet to come!

On the Workplace...
"Management is doing things right. Leadership is doing the right things."

-Peter Drucker

Chapter 5

The World of Work: From East to West

The world of work continues to be a great challenge for many women even though more opportunities have been made available than in years past. I have worked for and with a diverse group of individuals for over seventeen years. I have worked with many competent and talented men and women. However, as I look back over the years, it has become evident to me that a select group of people have gone the extra mile, extended the helping hand, offered advice and suggested strategies for me. These folks generally wore suits and ties. Matters of leadership, management, mentoring, business and politics have been topics of lunch meetings, emails, telephone consults, and office visits. Some discussions even took place in the homes of close friends and family members.

I think it is important to note that I have been diligent with pursuing my education and professional training. It has been equally important to me to have good work ethics, flexibility, a positive attitude and enormous faith. Along with my aspiration to move forward, I have been blessed to have met some remarkable people along the way. I have had several managers, but I distinctly remember those individuals with strong leadership abilities and how they managed to help me grow and develop. I am ever so grateful to those who gave me an opportunity to stretch my wings, increase my knowledge and enhance my skills. I have been blessed with a few guardian angels in suits during my brief journey in the world of work.

Darrell Caldwell

As I recall such experiences in the world of work, my first guardian angel was a gentleman in Austin, Texas. He was articulate, smart and he had a great sense of humor. What I remember most about his management style was his flexibility and concern for the success of his staff. He never said anything directly to me, but I knew he was sensitive to my situation. I was on the job for four months and my husband was out of the state on a temporary assignment for several months. Instantly, I became a temporary "single parent" of my baby girl, Kristen. He was also aware that I had recently moved to Texas from South Carolina and I did not have family or many friends in the area. This could have turned into a very bad situation. Instead, it became a very challenging and exciting time for me.

For example, during my late nights, I had the flexibility to pick up my daughter from childcare and bring her back to the office. This happened over ten years ago and most employers were not aiming for the "top ten family-friendly workplace" list. Yet, my supervisor was always encouraging me. He would often say, "Do what you need to do to get things done."

As the months passed, I found myself training new employees per his request. Later, I picked up added duties in our unit during his absence. We often had discussions about my future career plans, and he graciously gave me advice and provided excellent references over the years. This angel in a suit answers to the name, Darrell Caldwell. I worked for Darrell at the Travis County Juvenile Court from 1990–1992. Over the years, we have maintained contact and he continues to share words of encouragement from many miles away.

I share this encounter because so many women fall victim to unfair scrutiny because they are working mothers. Sometimes women are forced into difficult situations and find themselves making a choice between good parenting and working. I was blessed to have worked for someone with great character and wisdom. He saw my talents and abilities and chose to create an environment that would allow me to rise to the occasion.

I did not know much about him on a personal note but I knew he was a leader and team player. He wanted all of us to be successful as a unit. I do know that he was a father of two young girls and he was an active co-parent. Fortunately, he understood the challenges many employees faced with family responsibilities. Everyday, we saw the faces of many adolescents who did not receive the proper nurturing and care in their early years. Although I had my obstacles, he did not turn them into road blocks while working for him. *Darrell, I am forever grateful to you!*

Jack Gillbeaux

In 1992, we moved to Montgomery, Alabama when Chris was assigned to Maxwell Air Force Base. Once again, I found myself hitting the pavement to look for work. I searched for several months but used caution with exploration. I knew that I wanted to move forward but that it would be difficult in a new city without any contacts. In February 1992, I began working at a private non-profit agency. Initially, I enjoyed my work because I was in a new environment and I learned a lot about the dynamics of a non-governmental entity. However, as the months passed, I became bored and I was no longer challenged with my duties and responsibilities. Chris knew I was no longer happy with my work. I wanted to broaden my scope and increase my earnings. As I shared in Chapter 4, Chris was instrumental in securing my second position in Montgomery. Although he was dealing with his own ordeal at the base, he still considered my situation important and did what he could to make it better.

In July 1992, I began working at the Federation of Child Care Centers of Alabama (FOCAL) as the State Child Care Organizer. I was responsible for membership recruitment, visiting centers and interviewing center directors across the state. While working at FOCAL, I met Jack Guillbeaux. As we traveled across the state to various conferences and training sessions, I learned a great deal from him. Jack was tall with peppered-gray hair. He was a very wise man with a scholarly persona. He was very open about his life experiences and shared many lessons on civil rights and advocacy. I spent a lot of time around Jack but didn't talk to him much. I preferred to listen to him. It was always a treat. Jack encouraged me to think from a global perspective. He married a woman from Peru and his faith was rooted in Bahai. He traveled across the country and abroad. Upon return from his trips, he always had a life lesson or story to share. Jack was a mentor, teacher and friend. Although I did not work with him for very long, I was blessed to have met him.

Our time spent together was very valuable. I was a young and impressionable woman yearning to learn and discover better ways to work with children and families. His emphasis on history and human interaction was so striking. I had many "light bulb" experiences while listening to him as we traveled on the interstate. I am appreciative to him for his teachings. I will never forget the lessons learned on internalized oppression, cultural diversity and empowerment. As the author of *More is Caught than Taught: a Guide to Quality Child Care,* Jack will continue to positively influence the lives of many women as parents and teachers. This will ultimately bare fruit in the development of confident and empowered individuals. *Jack, thank you for taking the time to share!*

Geoffrey Williams

About six months after working at FOCAL, it was time to relocate again. We returned to South Carolina in 1994. It was time for resumes, classified ads and phone calls once again. Fortunately, I secured employment within a matter of weeks. It was at this job that I met two other gentlemen who had a positive impact on my professional and personal development. Geoffrey Williams was my immediate supervisor and Charles Pinckney was my coworker.

Geoffrey was spunky, full of humor and focused on quality service. He was a macro-manager and valued the ideas and opinions of his staff. I quickly learned that there was no blue print for the project, and it was an opportunity to speak up, be creative and make a mark. Fortunately, he was a manager with good listening skills and he answered questions with questions to push me even further. Although deadlines were important to him, he placed greater emphasis on the quality of the final product. He demonstrated his confidence in me and gave me space to do my job. He was attentive to staff wellness and showed concern for our success. Although we worked in a profession in which you dealt with constant client crisis, Geoffrey managed to keep office morale high and interjected frequent doses of humor and sunny sides to situations. As he discussed future plans of the project and our individual roles, he would often recognize my aspirations. He knew it would soon be time for me to move on for greater opportunities. He often shared his thoughts in a positive and encouraging manner. I never felt threatened or insecure about my status or role with the project because I knew he understood me. Yes, he knew as long as I was present that I would give one hundred percent but my eyes were on a bigger prize. He was an effective communicator and strived for effective communication among his subordinates. Geoffrey led by example.

Although many years have passed, we still get together a couple of times a year not to just catch up on things, but he gives me feedback and encouragement for whatever endeavor I take on. It has been eight years since our first encounter and I still look forward to our lunch meetings. This is a time when I can test out ideas before I take a leap. Geoffrey manages to ask a few questions for serious thought and then tops off our discussions with his special humor to remind me that we can be ambitious but we can laugh and have some fun along the way.

Charles Pinckney

Now, my relationship with Charles was very different. He was my coworker. We were forced to share office space together for several months. This was frightening to me. I had only worked a few years subsequent to completing college and I always had my own office space. All of a sudden, I found myself in a situation in which I was forced to share office space with a complete stranger who happened to be a man. I was in complete shock. This wasn't revealed during the interview. So, I wondered what other surprises would come my way.

My first inclination led me to think that this guy was going to push me around, and take the most valuable space. This felt like a deal that was going to go bad and go bad fast. Yet, I had later discovered that I had nothing to worry about. I was still in God's favor because he truly worked it out for me. As the weeks passed by, I learned a lot about Charles and discovered we had many things in common. We became an effective team and we also became good friends.

Charles was professional and enjoyed his work. He was trustworthy and reliable. He valued our teamwork and it was demonstrated consistently over the years. Our duties required home visits in various neighborhoods across Richland and Lexington counties. I could always depend on Charles to make good decisions about our safety practices. He made the extra effort to arrange his calendar to accommodate me. Many times, I did not have to ask for his assistance. He simply made the decisions accordingly. He would give sound advice, make observations and discuss courses of action to meet our goals. We had a good working relationship. We had this little joke going for awhile because several of his clients thought I was his secretary. He would play the part for awhile but later had to come correct. It was interesting to see how the minds of those young folks worked to make such quick assumptions about us. I don't think so! We were partners who respected each other and we played off of each other's strengths. Sure, when the first computer arrived, it found a home on my desk, but that was no big deal. I was doing a little more typing but I didn't make up the reports. We worked together as a team. That is what made it all work out.

Although we have parted ways in our careers, we still remain friends. I will never forget the way he respected me as a colleague and encouraged me to pursue entrepreneurial endeavors. I am very grateful for such a positive work experience. We were a team and we valued each other's talents and gifts. As I look back on the days of writing progress reports, I distinctly remember the sense of pride I felt as we documented our accomplished goals and efforts. We were an efficient team and we valued input from all members. There were opportunities to lead as well as follow.

Initially, I was concerned about the male dominance and wondered if attempts would be made to make me the silent team member and note keeper. Fortunately, I was placed in the presence of two gentlemen. Over the years, we have maintained friendships and continue to be motivators and encouragers to each other. *To Geoffrey and Charles, I say thank you!*

Benjamin Duncan, II

In 1997, I transitioned into the South Carolina State Government system. This was a very challenging time because I was temporarily a single parent and attending graduate school. I became employed at the Governor's Office and it was during that time I was encouraged and assisted by someone I knew from my hometown. Although I didn't know him very well, there was a kindred spirit between us. In that politicized environment, I began to learn the culture and rules of the game. Ben Duncan was very instrumental with my navigation of those governmental seas. His comments were brief

36

and concise. He didn't talk much and went straight to the point. He was always introducing me to people. His goal was to build my network. One day, he jokingly said to me, "Girl, you better get out and meet folks". I clearly understood his point. It was important to manage my time and get my work done. Yet, it was also imperative to get out of my workbox and develop relationships with other people. This would prove beneficial to me in days to come.

Ben so freely provided helpful tips and warnings. He steered me toward leadership opportunities, and he was consistent with his encouragement. Even during the bitter sweet days of the transition in the administration after the 1999 election, Ben seized an opportunity for me to stretch my wings. The Governor's Office needed someone to serve as the manager for the Leadership EXCEL Institute Class 98–99. I was a graduate of the preceding class and I thoroughly enjoyed the experience. I was flattered when Ben asked me to fill in the gap during the transition. Conducting the research and organizing the monthly sessions was an excellent opportunity for me. Although I was not monetarily compensated for these additional duties, there were several intangible benefits and I am appreciative.

He was never forceful with his ideas. He simply made inquiries and asked for my feedback. I had to make the decisions. Ben was not my supervisor and he was not a part of my chain of command. Yet, he quickly became a guardian angel. Our friendship developed over the years and I still seek his advice from time to time.

As time passed, I came to understand how his past experiences impacted many decisions he made and how those decisions ultimately defined his plotted course for achievement. Ben has always been inspired and motivated by his family. He wanted his family to be proud of him. Thus, he strived to excel. In his professional career, he has maintained a focus on having a competitive edge in the market. Although he has traveled through many peaks and valleys, he never lost his focus. He once shared with me that although he had specific goals as a youngster, he was forced to pursue a different professional journey due to physical health challenges. While faced with such limitations in his early adult life, that did not discourage him from excelling or helping others along the way. I am forever grateful to him for his friendship, advice and encouragement. Ben, you are appreciated. *Thanks for looking out for me!*

Calvin "Chip" Jackson

About three years later, I met another kind gentleman. Although we became acquainted during professional encounters, he became a guardian angel too. It was no secret that he was a man of faith and he openly shared his faith with me. It was evident that he enjoyed his work and he enjoyed life. As an executive level manager, he illuminated the hallway with energy and hope. As a staff member, I was motivated by his enthusiasm about work and life. I was always eager to listen to him as he revealed volumes of knowledge during our brief conversations. His wisdom was evident as he shared many life experiences and lessons learned. He constantly attempted to motivate me to seize every opportunity to plant seeds for the future.

I found it ironic that even though I had not known him very long, I felt connected to him. He quickly became another person I enjoyed listening to. No matter the topic of conversation, I became a sponge because I was certain I would learn something. I would always look forward to being in his presence.

Since his position included a wide span of control and he had a broad scope in responsibilities, our encounters were minimal and brief. Yet, those moments were treasured because he always checked in, guided and encouraged me. This was his nature with all of his employees. I witnessed the same dynamics with others, both male and female. As a manager, he strived to remain connected with his staff without becoming a micromanager. He was always asking questions and pushing for creativity. There was no fluff or frill. He was always very candid and he went straight to the point. Frequent words used in discussions included strategy, change, think, positioning, opportunity, future, absolutely and blessing.

I was intrigued by his high level of energy, intellect and drive. I wanted to learn more about him. I was very curious about his sources of motivation and how he acquired such a striking sense of confidence. (This was not to be confused with arrogance.) He was gracious and consented to sharing some personal experiences that gave insight to his growth, development and success. He described many special experiences about his childhood and family life. When I inquired about sources of motivation, he easily identified his paternal grandfather as a powerful motivator for him throughout the course of his life. At an early age, he learned many lessons from his grandfather, Andrew "Malcom" Jackson. Such lessons would have life long application for him. Self-confidence and assurance for success came from the seeds his grandfather planted in his heart and mind as a young boy. He explained that the manner in which he interacts with people and conducts business stems from his grandfather's teaching. He described his grandfather as a man of strength and vision. He reared four children as a single parent during challenging times for African-American families. Yet, this extraordinary man gave even more to his grandchildren and made a life lasting impression upon this particular grandson, Calvin "Chip" Jackson.

After Chip shared excerpts of his experiences, it became clearer to me how and why he is the way he is. He has deep roots of family values, work ethics and faith. Such a combination can only result in development of a compassionate, enthusiastic and determined individual. He makes you believe that you can do anything. You can succeed! Thus, he has been a great source of motivation to me. He has challenged me to do better and to do more. He always pushes one with questions. He knows his thoughts and positions on certain issues but wants to know if you know them. You can see it in his eyes when he poses the question. He's waiting for you to say it. Then when he hears it, there is a distinct affirmative nod of the head to let you know your response was the answer he was waiting to hear.

I know that Calvin "Chip" Jackson was an angel placed in my life to help me even further on my journey. I am thankful for the opportunity to have joined his team and I value his friendship. He always has encouraging words to share. He's very intuitive and seems to always find a scripture or life experience to shed light on a situation. I have learned a great deal from him, and I know that he has always had my best interest at heart just as he does for others. I know that I can always count on him for professional advice as well as spiritual guidance. *Chip, I recognized the Jabez appointment and I am forever thankful! You are a constant reminder of the plight to "be blessed and be a blessing to others".*

Truly Blessed

Since 1985, I have been employed in many different places. I am grateful for all of my experiences across the country from the east to the west and back to South Carolina.

I have met many people from different walks of life. Although I have established some solid relationships with female colleagues and even made some wonderful friends, it has been my experience that those who have advised me the most and even created opportunities for me to excel were my "angels in suits". I have been very fortunate to have not experienced any degrees of sexual harassment, discrimination as a working mother or any other forms of workforce injustices as a female. Unfortunately, this is not the testimony of all women. Many sisters continue to endure unfair treatment and have been victimized at some point on the journey. In those instances, I hope that my sisters will be able to step forward and pursue justice. However, for those angels in suits that continue to strive to help women and men excel to make their dreams a reality, I salute them! I am inspired to keep moving forward and help others when I can. For those of you who are willing to help, take the step, even if it is a small step. We all have goals and dreams. I understand that it is important to remain focused and eliminate factors of distraction to pursue our goals. However, it is conceivable for women to incorporate the tier of assistance to other sisters in the master plan. For those of you who have had similar experiences, I encourage you to share your guardian angels and be grateful. Share your story and reach back to help others.

On Advice...
"All of us, at certain moments of our lives, need to take advice and receive help from other people."
-Alexis Carrell, Reflections on Life

Chapter 6:

Coaching on the Sidelines

I cannot complete this tribute without acknowledging another group of "suits" that have coached me from the sidelines. I did not have formal working relationships with them and they were not members of my extended family. Instead, they managed to coach me from a distance. With their own unique role and individual style, these men have greatly influenced many decisions I have made over the years. The encouragement and motivation I received from them have been priceless. In many respects, they have been unaware of the magnitude of their influence. Therefore, I am taking this opportunity to say thank you.

As I reflect back over the years, my mind floats back and focuses on these special coaches that shared their play book on life with me. My coaches were Willie Wade Davis, the late William B. James, and John E. Miles. Many times, I failed to let them know how much their coaching helped me cross the finish line in victory. I am sure you will agree that these are some special folks.

Willie Wade Davis

Willie Wade Davis is a native of Winnsboro, South Carolina, and he is one of eleven siblings. Davis was the third born child but the oldest brother. His father died when he was thirteen. Upon graduation from high school, he worked in a local plant for a short period of time. However, after an episode of verbal abuse and being the timely scapegoat for some damaged material, he knew that was a work environment he could not tolerate. Although the plant owner visited him at home to ask him to return to the job, Davis declined the offer because the owner could not guarantee civil behavior of the supervisor. Subsequently, Davis enlisted into the U.S. Army. He attributes his path to military service because he saw no future in Winnsboro. Upon graduation from basic training, he completed his three years of service and returned to Winnsboro. Unfortunately, about twenty-five miles outside of Winnsboro on his journey back home, the transmission in his car died. So he basically made it back to his mom's house at a snail's pace. He was home about two weeks and could not find a job. Davis was unemployed with a broken down car and no money. Unannounced, a friend from Orange, Texas, who served with him in the army, came through South Carolina to visit with him a few days. His friend was on his way to Fort Campbell to re-enlist in the army. While his friend hung around Winnsboro a few days, the thought never crossed his mind to return to the army and his friend never asked him to go with him. However, as Davis helped his friend load the car that special morning, it hit him. He went back in the house to get his duffle bag. Ironically, he had never completely unpacked. With such a short notice, his mother was not happy. She thought it was not a good idea for him to go back into the army and jump out of planes on purpose. She was not happy! Air Born was the destiny. Davis said, "The Lord sent Joe by my house. There were plenty of ways he could have gone to Fort Campbell." Upon re-enlistment in the army, Davis and Joe were assigned to the same company. There was no looking back after that. After a total of twenty-one years of service, Davis retired from the army in 1976. He shared that the most challenging obstacle during his military career was to watch others that did less get the promotions. Davis said, "I excelled at soldering and doing the job." However, his source of motivation came from other black men who were up against the problem. They encouraged each other and challenged each other. He said, "Your father was one of them. I guess maybe he needed a brother and I needed a brother even though I had five brothers and he had two. The Lord decided that." Davis and my father became good friends. He revealed that he really enjoyed traveling to visit my dad's father, Andrew Hill, in Columbus, Georgia. My grandfather treated him like a son and a friend. Grandfather shared some things with him that he would not share with his sons. They talked about a lot of things. He said that they (he and dad) shared my grandfather. That statement only confirmed my long time sense of kinship to him. Here is a brief sketch of our journey together.

My childhood memories are filled with episodes of this tall towering man with the biggest smile that one could ever imagine. Although he is not related to me by blood, I am closer to him than I have ever been to any of my uncles. His influence has not stemmed from what he told me but what he showed me.

Often times he was assumed to be my father's brother and it always saddened me just a little to say, "No, he's my dad's friend." Although I loved him like family, he was "Sgt. Davis". After he retired from the Army, I didn't know what to call him. Several years later I began to refer to him as "Uncle Wade". From childhood to adulthood, I learned a great deal from him. My biggest lesson was about friendship. He was my dad's best friend as far back as I can remember. Today, I am amazed at the longevity and depth of their friendship. Sure, they are old army buddies. Yet, as the years progressed beyond military careers, I saw in him traits of consistency, reliability, loyalty, love and compassion.

No matter what was going on in his life with family, work, politics and other things, he was always a good friend. Through graduations, weddings, sickness and deaths, he was always there for my father and our family. I often think of the times that I was in need of some form of assistance and his answer was always "yes, I'll be there". He has always been nurturing and encouraging. He loved me like one of his girls. On February 3, 1986, my paternal grandfather died. It was a long drive from Sumter to Columbus. As I pulled in front of my grandmother's house, there were many cars parked in the yard and along the street. Yet, I distinctly remember the first car I recognized belonged to Davis. I thought to myself, what a wonderful friend. He came to be with my father during such a difficult time and he came quickly. At the time, I did not have a clue about the relationship Davis had with my grandfather nor did I really understand the depth of his friendship to my father and our family. However, I did have time to reflect back on the times in which he served as surrogate father to me and my older sister. One year, my sister was preparing for her big debutante ball in Sumter and my father was in Germany. This was a major bad deal for my sister because in addition to giving her away at her wedding, my father was supposed to escort her on the night she was to be formerly introduced to the community. Yes, Davis came to Sumter to stand in for my father. He came to town fully equipped with his tuxedo and that million dollar smile to properly escort my sister.

All my life, I have admired his willingness to come and

be a part of our family. He showed us what real friendship is all about. Even as an adult, with my husband overseas and my dad out of town, I found myself stranded on the side of the road outside of Columbia destined to be late for work. (Of course, my cars conveniently break down at the most inappropriate times.) Davis was just a phone call away. With husband gone, I immediately thought of Daddy. Then when I realized that Daddy was out of town on business, I automatically thought of Davis. Yes, he came to the rescue.

As I look back over the years, it is not the frequent times of assistance that mark my heart but his ability to demonstrate the wealth in one's life through friendship. He has shown me how true friendships can be assets, personally and professionally. He has defied all accounts of jealousy, back stabbing and other shortcomings that manage to destroy friendships and limit opportunities in life. It is all about healthy relationships and being true to a friend.

I asked him if he had any advice for young people striving to excel in life and he said, "Knowing yourself and what you're capable of is very critical. You shouldn't be floating around. When God is in your life, it's much better. Better sooner than later so you won't have so many patches in your life. I recommend having a good friend in your life that will tell you like it is and that you can be the same type of friend. Be real."

Uncle Wade, I love you very much and really appreciate all that you have shared with me and my family. I have learned a true lesson from you! Thank you for your continued prayers and encouragement.

Willie Wade Davis
Vietnam, 1968

Young army buddies, Davis and my father in
Korea in 1960.

John E. Miles

John E. Miles was born in Florence County, South Carolina and raised in the surrounding area. He attended elementary school in Lake City and dropped out of school in the seventh grade. He later went back to pursue eighth grade but it didn't work out. At the age of 16, John joined the US Army. It was a way out. He shared with me that one of his greatest sources of motivation was survival. However, the Army was not only an avenue for survival but a venue to excel. John did exceptionally well in school while in the army. Things really began to take off for him. After his enlistment in the Army, John became involved in politics and ran for a seat in the SC House of Representatives. Elected in 1972, he served one term. In 1976, he was elected to the SC Senate and served for four years. In1978, he earned an undergraduate degree at the University of South Carolina and subsequently graduated from the USC School of Law in 1981. He began his private practice in Sumter in 1981 and the rest is history. John is a legend of his own time. His journey includes time spent as a general manager in broadcasting, public servant, lawyer, and community activist. He has written a wonderful collection of poetry but has never published his work.

For many years, I have marveled at the drive, motivation and intellect of this man. He has a brilliant mind and incredible style. If you are interested in learning something, take some time to listen to him talk. He even has a subtle shade of humor in the most controversial topics of discussion. Although our encounters have been irregular and brief over the years, he has given me sound advice, encouragement and a degree of inspiration to excel and achieve. One day, I hope to read his complete biography and some of his poetry. He is a remarkable human being.

I really appreciate his willingness to spare me some of his time over the years. Now, let me tell you a little about our journey together....

When I walked into his office for the first time, I was really curious. His set up was much like every other law office I visited. There was a general reception area with a few desks sprinkled along side two walls. It seemed to be an average small town practice. After being properly greeted, John was notified that I was in the waiting area. Within a matter of minutes, my perception about him and his practice changed completely. As I briskly walked to the back of the first floor and elevated up the stairs to the second floor, I felt as though I had stepped into the twilight zone. It seemed as though I had leaped into a different time and place. I said to myself, "Wow! Oh my God!" His collection of art, books, photographs and other items were breath taking. I was obviously in the presence of a brilliant and talented man. He was not your average lawyer. This guy had skills, mega brain power, and years of experience.

After the slap of reality, I came to my senses and decided that whatever he had to say, I would listen attentively. He spoke with a quick pace and a colorful vocabulary. He shifted topics with ease. Instantly, I knew that if I had a second visit, a tape recorder would come in handy. His quotes from Socrates, Aristotle, and Shakespeare were astonishing. All the while, I was praying I could keep up with him and not say anything stupid. Of course, I was intimidated initially but he later became my friend and advisor. I learned a lot from John.

When I met him, his appearance and demeanor easily misled me to believe he came from a family lineage of elite status and long money. Yet, after talking with him for only a few minutes, I quickly became inspired by his remarkable story. His life experiences come complete with tremendous challenges and accomplishments. He is quick to tear down the big myths that keep so many people from even attempting to excel in life. As he simply states, "It is one's own fear and perception that other people or things hold them back. Therefore, if it is believed in one's heart and mind, then there is no reason to try."

On many occasions, John has attempted to persuade me to go to law school. Often times, he emphasized the high rate of divorce rate in this country and expressed his concern for so many women with children who find themselves struggling to survive. He is convinced that having the ability to practice law can assure a woman's livelihood and security. I have no idea how many times he has shared this scenario with me, but it struck a cord with me. Of course John has always said he wished for me many years of happiness and adventure in marriage. However, he has seen so many families impacted by differences and mothers' lack of ability to provide a quality life for their children. Although he hasn't completely persuaded me to go to law school yet, he continues to have my ear to listen and learn from what he's willing to share.

Unknowingly, John has coached me from a distance, and it is important to me to properly recognize his influence over the years. His role as legal counsel, mentor and friend has carved a deep imprint in my heart forever. Oh yes, how could I forget? I can't even count the amount of money I have saved from consulting and confiding in him over the years.

A quarterly visit to his law office is certain to boost my energy level and keep me motivated to pursue my goals. Yes, he might tell a good joke and spend a few minutes with small talk, but you can rest assured that I cannot leave his office without a true lesson in history, politics, or law.   The wonderful thing about it all is that I know that there is nothing special about me. It is all about what a special person he is. John has spent many years giving to his community and making a difference for people who cannot afford legal services. He even kicks in generous amounts of financial donations to causes in the community. I know this first hand because my mom often strolls in his office with her hands out with a special request. He graciously heeds to her request. He has been a good friend to my parents for years, and I have been fortunate enough to reap the benefits. I am not exactly sure how and when they developed their friendship, but I can assure you that I have been observing and learning from John for many years.

John, thank you for taking the time and being willing to share! I appreciate all that you do. (It is always good to have a brilliant lawyer in your corner!)

William B. James

The late William B. "Pop" James was born on January 10, 1903. He was educated in Sumter and graduated from Morris College in 1926. He was a public school teacher, principal and education advisor to the Civilian Conservation Corp.   Later, he enrolled in Robert Terrell Law School in Washington, D.C. and earned his law degree in 1947. He returned to his native town and practiced law until 1954 when his family relocated to the D.C. area. Squire James, as he was called by many Sumterites, lived an adventurous and controversial life to be remembered by many for years to come. He was a civil rights activist, attorney, and family man.   In 1949,

*he was the first black lawyer since Reconstruction to argue a case before the South Carolina Supreme Court. In 1960, he was the first black attorney of the Federal Trade Commission and later became a senior attorney for the Commission's Office of Consumer Complaints in the District of Columbia. In 1971, he retired and returned to Sumter in 1975. It was during this time that he adopted my family as his own and I developed a very special relationship with him. He was fondly called **Pop James**. From 1975 until his death in 1989, Pop continued his journey as a civil rights activist, community leader and political consultant. In 1999, he was posthumously inducted into the South Carolina Black Hall of Fame. One can only imagine how he has influenced my thinking and decisions over the years. As I have grown older, I have developed an even greater appreciation for his personal influence as well as his contributions to our society.*

Our time together began during my adolescent years. When I think of Pop James, I laugh because he was a tough old guy. He didn't like much that interested me. Things that were synonymous to youth included television, radio, telephone and simply having fun. For Pop, he had other things for us to do. The list began with reading, proper diction and etiquette. He was really tough to be around at times. I knew he loved me and I could handle him for little spurts at a time. As I grew older, he got tougher. He didn't like any of my boyfriends, didn't want me to have a car while attending college, and he constantly preached about education. Underneath that tough lawyer was a warm heart full of love and hope for generations to come. He would talk for hours about racism, politics and leadership. Some of the stories he shared seemed too cruel to be true. I remember the story of the cross burning in his yard before he returned to D.C. I guess he was kicking up too much of the truth, so he had to be harassed by some of the small thinking members of the community.

During my teen years, I could only tolerate so much about district lines, party affiliation and the likes. Yet, as I look back over the years, I am grateful that he took the time to help me understand what was going on and how it would impact my future. I often think of the days when most of his conversations centered on the landmark case of *Blanding vs. Dubose*. In 1978, Pop represented the Public Awareness Association and filed a law suit against Sumter County. It was a lengthy legal battle that lasted until 1984. The U.S. Supreme Court ordered that Sumter County change its method of elections from the at-large method to the single-member district method. "On June 8, 1984, the Public Awareness Association celebrated the decision of a three-judge federal court panel which found that the at-large method of electing Sumter County Council members discriminated against blacks and was not in compliance with the Voting Rights Act" (Morris, 1989, p.63). Those long boring conversations with him at age fourteen later became eye opening discussions that would matter to me many years to come as a citizen, voter, parent, public servant and tax payer. I learned a lot sitting at his knee.

He would often share books and papers with me to read as I talked about school assignments. My parents valued education and Pop James was their frontline reinforcement. When I came home from college on the weekends, he was eager to discuss my grades and progress in school. I had complete access to his personal library. Being in his presence was an educational campground. He had lots of old books, papers and newspaper articles. He freely gave of his time and energy. Pop had tough love! He would say things and not dress it up. It simply came out of his mouth straight from the heart. As a teenager, I really didn't understand why he was so controversial. Yet, as an adult, I grew to appreciate his contributions to the community and his impact on my life. *Pop, I know you are still watching over me. I miss you very much!*

Pop James in his younger
days before he entered my life.
(Date unknown)

On Motherhood....
"Teach your children to choose the right path, and when they are older, they will remain upon it."
-Proverbs 31:29

My parents, Anthriest Hill, Sr. and Frances D. Hill
Sumter, South Carolina 2000

Chapter 7:

Special Edition: Suit without a Tie

*M*any women have given birth to children but all of them are not mothers. Yet, I know that God favored me with a very special mother. Let me briefly explain how I came to this conclusion. She was born and raised in Sumter, South Carolina. She was the daughter of a farmer and a domestic worker. Surviving the struggle of black families with limited economic and civic opportunity, she discovered the journey of hard work by picking cotton with her siblings before and after school. She graduated from Lincoln High School in 1957 and attended Northeastern University in Boston, Massachusetts.

In 1966, she returned to her hometown. As a military wife, she quickly mastered the mystical art of working and caring for three children with her husband miles away. Her ability to balance family and work while remaining active in her community was a significant accomplishment to me. She symbolized strength and determination that I later came to value very much. Although there are far too many to mention, let me share a few descriptors to illustrate the depth of her inner strength. In 1971, she received her Lay Speaker Certification from the United Methodist Church and in 1977, she became a certified Lay Speaker Instructor for the South

Carolina United Methodist Conference. In addition to her activism in the church, she also remained involved in other facets of the community. She was the first African-American to serve as the PTA President for Millwood Elementary School and the first African-American woman to serve as the President for the Sumter Civitan Club whereby she received the Outstanding Honor Club Achievement Award. She also served on a variety of local boards and commissions. In 1990, she was honored by the YWCA Tribute to Women and Industry for outstanding work in the community. Ruby Johnson, Executive Director of the Wateree Community Actions, Incorporated, has captured her essence by writing, "she is reputed to be forceful and demanding to obtain what she seeks. As a driving force, she has opened many a door to resources for poor people, as well as for her employer.

Frances is strong on poor people receiving what they are entitled to, and she is equally strong on motivating the poor to take advantage of opportunities to lift themselves above poverty...Her liberal giving of time and possessions to the many memberships she holds, to Wateree Community Actions, to her church and to the community and poor people's causes has dubbed her a humanitarian of note."

I recall many folks calling her "Killer Hill" during my childhood. I never really knew how she inherited that nickname, but she once told me that Retired Chief Justice Ernest Finney, Jr. gave her that name and it stuck with her. So when I began working on this project, I wanted to inquire about it further and get it straight from the source. As a long time family friend, he was gracious enough to take a little time and tell me about the origination of such a nickname for my mom. When I asked him why he coined that name for her, he quickly recalled how it came to pass as though it were only yesterday. He sternly stated that, "It was an attribution to her strong will. She didn't take any slack and she had a killer personality. She called a spade a spade and when she said something, she would follow through." I immediately recalled incidents that *matched each descriptor he raised. It all added up. He knew my mother, her ways and her intent.*

As a child, the nickname seemed odd to me. Yet, as an adult, I have an appreciation for her unique style, and I admire Chief Justice Finney for his wit to coin such a nickname to capture her power. Thus, one can only imagine the impact she has had on my growth and development as a woman, Christian, mother, wife and community member. My mom, Frances D. Hill, is another guardian angel who has protected, nurtured and guided me all of my days. Let me share some of the highlights of her influence over the years.

Now, this angel routinely wore suits but never with a tie. She chose to accent her suits with an endless collection of fancy shoes. She was small in stature but stood tall with dignity and confidence. She was loving, generous and filled with compassion. Yet, she ruled with a firm hand. She was a magician and had the ability to vanish the word "no" when responding to her requests. However, she would never ask something of someone that she would not do herself. She stood just above five feet, but it was a tall order to fill her shoes. She never served in the military but she was tough, disciplined and demanded great effort. By some, she will be remembered for her resounding "Amen" when in agreement with the word. Others will always remember her love for community and her constant desire to help other people. Some will always remember her resourcefulness and her ability to make things happen. Yet, I will always remember her constant love, protection, support, and guidance. My mother's big heart, warm hugs and strong hands will always remain in my mind's eye. She defined womanhood, motherhood and friendship for me.

Over the years, I have watched her love and care for many friends and family members. I have learned a great deal from her about service to others with no strings attached. She taught me to value education, independence and family. To me, my mother has always symbolized strength and determination. I have watched her cry, shout, laugh and rejoice. Her unwavering faith in God and assurance has transcended upon me. I have realized that when I see the easy route to giving up, my inner strength and determination takes over to help me keep going.

My mom would often tell us the stories of picking cotton early in the mornings before school, and again after school. She shared lessons learned and values gained for family, work, and helping others. Although she came up through tough times, she wanted the best for us. Mom always hammered us to "do your best, do it right or do it over." She often spoke of difficult times during the civil rights movement era. She generously shared lessons learned for life application in the present time. I remember her as a big helper during my childhood. I can't remember her ever helping me with my school work but she insists that she did. However, I do recall children from other families coming over for tutoring sessions. She would sit at the dining room table with school books, papers, pencils, and encyclopedias. Our dining room was frequently turned into a learning sanctuary for many children. Those images became permanent imprints in my mind.

I also remember another entity near and dear to her heart. She had a great love for the Girl Scouts at First Baptist Church on Washington Street. She would drag me along with her every Monday after school even though I was not old enough to participate in the troop's activities. Finally, I became a Brownie. Then, for twelve consecutive years, we journeyed to Girls Scouts together. She continued her service there years after I graduated from high school.

In addition to her love for helping young people, she was very active in her church and the faith community. She became commonly known as the "Amen Lady". She loved to sing and listen to the word. During my childhood, I remember sitting on the church pew with her and my grandmother. My grandmother would often lean towards her and whisper, "Sing a song, Fran." As an adult, I often tease my mother because she can't hit those high notes like she used to during her early thirties. Yet, she still enjoys whirling out a tune every now and then.

Other distinct memories include her frequent visits to the sick and elderly. As a young child, I was hauled around in the back seat of the car to travel down long country roads to see old relatives and friends. This seemed to bring great joy to my grandmother, but it bored me to tears. My mother would sit on the side of the bed and feed them. We would have prayer and even sing to them. Although this was a boring routine for me as a child, I later came to appreciate her sense of compassion and kindness to others with no strings attached.

As the years passed, many things became clearer in my mind. I came to recognize that she laid the foundation for me to stand strong in the face of hardships as an adult. As a military wife for thirteen years, I found myself seeking comfort and support from her. She also served as a sounding board for me for the daily challenges working women encounter, and she became a motivator as we moved around the country. During exciting times and difficult times, she has always been there for me.

My mother also taught me the importance of staying informed and involved. She emphasized the importance of maintaining a strong presence in my child's school and other facets of her life. As an empowered parent, I can effectively advocate on my daughter's behalf just as my mom did for me.

As she gracefully moves into her senior years, she continues to advise, motivate and nurture me. Often times, I find myself doing things I saw her do when I was a child. Although we are very different, we have a great deal in common. I used to pick at her about being involved in community, civic and political activities. At the time, I was simply immature and lacked vision. Today, it's not so funny because I see more of my mother in myself. My mother, Frances Dicks Hill, has been a constant positive force in my life. She has always had my back and my best interest at heart. She's been a guardian angel all of my life and I am forever grateful to her.

Recognizing that mothers have such powerful roles in the development of strong and confident women, I salute all mothers who have given their best to set standards, lead by example and continue to encourage their daughters. I do realize that due to various circumstances, there are many broken and/or fragmented mother-daughter relationships. It is my prayer that relationships will be mended or even established. For those who cannot go back and the future is with your own young daughter, I pray that you will be inspired and encouraged to cultivate a strong and healthy relationship as well as reach out to those young ladies who are motherless. It will take strong women to help develop future generations of strong women. *Mom, I love you dearly. I appreciate everything you have done for me since I entered the world. Stay forever strong!*

My mother, Frances D. Hill
Sumter, South Carolina 1970

On Making a Difference...
"Act as if what you do makes a difference. It does."
-William James

Chapter 8:

The Quest: What Can I Do?

I have been truly blessed over the years. I look back over the miles I have traveled and recall all of the peaks and valleys. So far, it has been a challenging but good journey. I look forward to my future with great expectations. I am full of hope and faith. I am grateful for those that have passed my way and took the time to be kind, helpful and full of encouragement. As I have shared such recollections and observations with other female friends and colleagues, I have learned that many of them have had very similar experiences. Many of their advisors and mentors have been men. I have even discovered more about this dynamic as I participated in focus groups with local organizations. This discovery became an affirmation for me that I was not alone and that I need to be a part of the solutions to make things different for women. It did not matter how small my contribution or how little the impact. I felt compelled to take action. Thus, my quest for taking action was created.

Today, I find myself feeling closer to reaching goals I set very long ago. Yet, I find myself ascertaining new goals for the future. Pondering thoughts on business, politics, education and philanthropy, I find hope in my past experiences and feel certain that I will continue to meet people strategically placed in my life to guide, protect and encourage me.

However, I am still saddened and discouraged by the weak links between many young women striving to progress in the workplace and the community. Yet, I remain motivated to make a difference. I want to share experiences with other women and become a source of encouragement to them. I gave much time and thought to create a solution that I could live with and be able to look in the mirror without shame.

In the fall of 2001, I was inspired to create a network for young aspiring women to share and support each other. Finding very little value in male bashing, I sought to bring women together to discuss common experiences and create strategies to help each other accomplish goals. Creating an opportunity to access information and resources was also imperative. I am committed to making this happen for myself and other women.

As the founder of the Support Your Sister (SYS) Network, I am committed to making my vision a reality. I have extended personal invitations to several talented women with special strengths and gifts. I hope that this network will continue to be a forum for sharing, feedback, problem solving and support for women who dare to dream. By cultivating relationships, women will have a strong voice and can impact outcomes that affect them individually and collectively. Today, I encourage women to step out of the box, take risks, and come together. I am hopeful for the days to come when women become stronger and better connected to each other.

Several months ago, I discussed my plans with a friend, Sharon Mills Pinckney, and she shared an interesting experience with me. A few years ago, she divorced and became a single parent. After recognizing the need for a forum for single mothers in her community, she created a support group. Although she had envisioned a place for women to discuss common challenges and discover mechanism to overcome the challenges, her first session was ignited with a few individuals attempting to discuss their past relationships and gravitate towards a male bashing session. Fortunately, she was able to steer the group back on its course and re-iterate the purpose of the group. It has been a couple of years and the group continues to meet. Even though the group has met its challenges and encountered peaks and valleys, it is still an opportunity for mothers to network and support each other. The same can be true in the world of work and politics. Although we are living in different times, women who have succeeded at beating the odds can offer so much to young women pursuing goals. I know that organizing and allowing structured time for women to come together and discuss issues are very valuable and effective strategies.

The SYS Network began meeting in December 2001. Because of schedule conflicts, it was difficult for everyone to meet at one time. Thus, we were constantly meeting new people because different folks showed up each time. I wasn't concerned about the numbers but wanted to make sure that our time was well spent for those who attended. The energy has been amazing. By the summer, my vision was a reality. We were sharing goals and hobbies as well as discovering commonalities.

During our gatherings, issues of work, school, relationships, and health were raised at various times. It was very encouraging to see women quickly connect with experiences, and offer suggestions to consider. The group is still small and functions in informal manners. I really believe that great things are headed our way!

As the network provides additional support for me and my peers, I can continue to explore other opportunities to make a difference for others. Such avenues to explore include becoming a mentor for someone in my workplace in addition to my participation in the Leader2leader Project. Seeking out formal opportunities for leadership development as well as political activism have been areas of consideration. I do not have any specific plan of action and defined time line at this point. However, I realize that it is coming soon. I must simply take an inventory and outline my priorities. Subsequently, I will need to assess my resources, strengths and weaknesses, and establish some action steps. I know that with the support of my network and the continued guidance from my angels in suits, I will be well on my way to achieving my goals.

This past year has been an awesome time. I have been taking the time to plan, connect and reflect with other sisters. A couple of my sisters from the network have shared with me that I have been a source of encouragement to them. I was really moved by their remarks because I didn't feel as if I had done anything that would bare fruit so soon. They made my heart glad and certainly motivated me to stay focused on the mission of the network. I hope that my sharing will encourage others to join me in this quest! *To my sisters of the SYS Network; stay forever strong! To Melissa Lindler and Trina Randle; your words continue to ring in my ears and keep me focused!*

On Action...
"Never mistake motion for action."
-Ernest Hemmingway (1863-1947)

Chapter 9:

A Call for Action: What Can Women Do?

This call for action will require the exploration of major issues women face, current trends and opportunities. Today, women face many obstacles that include lack of role models, mentors, and support mechanisms. Our desires to compete sometimes outweigh our desire and abilities to assist other women. It is crucial for us to begin searching for ways to maintain our competitive edge while aiding others in attaining higher heights. Self-confidence and a willingness to take risks are tools needed to meet the challenge. However, we must be willing to stand with other sisters and combat these issues in a strategic manner.

Current trends indicate an increase in CEO positions held by women in the corporate world but there is still great room for further advancement. In the world of politics, women tend to be a significant portion of the voting population, yet we are underrepresented in elected capacities. In recent years, several groups across the country have been created to unite women and establish a collective voice to impact elections. Many groups have developed missions to identify and support women candidates at various levels.

Another effective mechanism for progression is networking.   This wealth of resources is underutilized by women.   Many groups have been established to bring women together for networking opportunities.   Various groups have specific areas of focus to exchange information such as job leads and support.   It is a great opportunity for women to come together to build teamwork skills and enhance leadership abilities.   In addition to regular meetings and planned events, women often utilize electronic networks to share information and tips.

As women concentrate on career tracks and strategies for advancement, it is crucial to utilize resources for skill building, mentoring, and career development.   Accessing information and exploring strategies are key factors for good decision making.   Thus, having an opportunity to make sound and informed decisions is imperative.

As women make decisions regarding professional advancement, many of us are faced with the challenge of balancing work and family.   While women are still trying to level the field, it is important to have support mechanisms in place for women to address the challenges of the balancing act.   Many women make career choices based upon their family circumstances and in many instances it limits opportunities to pursue preferred career tracks.

Although women make up approximately fifty percent of the workforce, there is a small percentage of women in high level management and executive positions.   As women strive to migrate into this untapped territory, networks and support groups will meet the need to aid in the advancement of women.

I am often baffled by the discussions with older women who share their experiences about college and their chosen profession.   During the 1950's and 1960's, there were limited career choices for women as well as opportunities for leadership roles.   Many women have shared that as they prepared for college, their parents encouraged them to get a formal education and plan to become a teacher, nurse or secretary. Today, we have many more options due to the sacrifices of others over the years. Yet, women are underrepresented in elected positions and executive management positions within major companies across the country.

As I look at the state of South Carolina, I am amazed at the minimal number of women in leadership positions in state government and in the private sector. Yes, women have made significant progress over the years, but we still have an unleveled playing field. Women must come together and take action. We have some good advocates both male and female but more help is needed.

While I am grateful for those individuals who make a conscientious effort to promote capable and qualified women to lead and manage major agencies and businesses, there is a need for women to rise up and command additional opportunities. I encourage our women leaders to share their time and talents with the aspiring young women.

As I inquired about these issues with colleagues, friends, and community leaders, I was amazed at the lack of female mentors. It caused me to reflect back on my own experiences only to find that I too lacked the opportunity to interact with a woman mentor. Of course I previously shared my mother's influence, and she has certainly been a mentor in various respects. However, from a formal and professional angle, I have lacked the mentoring experience. I have learned much from previous female supervisors but not in the capacity as a mentor.

Therefore, the question is presented to women to resolve this obstacle for women. I strongly believe that women must create opportunities to network, build coalitions, support each other and serve as mentors. There is a great need for us to share experiences, offer encouragement, cultivate friendships and utilize resources. Women must seek out opportunities and resources at various institutions to include colleges, churches and government. We are all called to get involved, stand up and speak out!

On Leadership...
"Leadership is not so much about technique and methods as it is about opening the heart. Leadership is about inspiration—of oneself and of others. Great leadership is about human experiences, not processes. Leadership is not a formula or a program, it is an activity that comes from the heart and considers the hearts of others. It is an attitude, not a routine."
-Lance Secretan

Chapter 10:

Leap into Leadership

As we examine where women are today in leadership roles, we must be mindful of how opportunities are created for women to demonstrate their leadership abilities. Women can be effective leaders in politics, communities, and businesses. However, as we socialize our young women, it becomes imperative to create opportunities for leadership development at an early age. Nurturing and empowering young women will cultivate a field of strong and self-confident women who will ultimately become effective leaders.

During my research, I discovered some astounding facts about the status of women in South Carolina and across the country. The Center for American Women and Politics at Rutgers University reported that in 2001, South Carolina ranked forty-eight in the number of women elected to the state legislature. The legislature was composed of 10.6% of women in 2001 and in 2000. While in 1999, women made up 11.2% and 12.9% in 1998. From 1975 to 2001, the percent of women elected to the state legislature has never exceeded 12.9%.

Furthermore, during the summer of 2001, I participated in a focus group at Columbia College for the Leadership Institute and discovered that many women identified with the same obstacles and challenges I had encountered. Under the leadership of Dr. Linda Salane, the study brought many facts to the forefront for interested women and the community. The information gathered from the focus group will be used to guide the Leadership Institute in its efforts to support women in leadership as well as prepare young women for leadership roles.

After the conclusion of the study, Dr. Salane shared the results with me as well as the results from a similar study conducted at Harvard in 2001. In essence, the statistics from a national and local perspective were disheartening. The report revealed that less than twelve percent of Fortune 500 corporate officers are women and five Fortune 500 CEO's were women. From a local perspective, the study found that South Carolina ranks near last in the number of women on boards and the number of women CEO's.

As the results of this study were compared with the results of a similar study at Harvard, it was an affirmation for me that there is a distinct dynamic occurring with women. I knew I was not crazy. No longer do I ask myself, "Is it just me?'. The findings of the two studies were insightful.

The Harvard Study identified several major challenges for women that included gender stereotypes, limited networks, few role models and problems of work/home balance. We know what the problems and challenges are for women. Now, our efforts should focus on designing a solution and recruiting others to join the effort.

So, how do we shift the tide and increase opportunities for women? I offer the following steps for consideration. One, increase awareness as a starting point. Two, women must band together and support each other's interest and aspirations. Three, women must allow themselves to be available to mentor other women. Four, women must actively create and participate in events to aid with skill development and enhancement. Five, women must align themselves with men that support their efforts and learn from them when possible. Six, women must remain informed and involved in policy development and practices that impact their status. These are just a few suggestions for women to consider what and how they can contribute to leveling the playing field. Women must get in the game and play to win!

I have already encountered some women warriors who are making a difference in South Carolina and impacting the world. It has been my privilege to meet these dynamic women who are champions for women in leadership. God has blessed me to become closely acquainted with Linda Salane, Director of the Leadership Institute at Columbia College; and Vicki Brown, Program Coordinator for the Leadership Institute. They have been true motivators, teachers and supporters. I have seen them in action and I admire their passion. I enjoy being in their presence and have benefited from their strategic efforts to make a difference for women in South Carolina and around the globe.

I distinctly remember how our journey together began as though it were yesterday. One afternoon, I went seeking resources from them but received more than I could have ever imagined. During the spring of 2001, I visited the Center for Women Entrepreneurs and met Vicki. Sure, she gave me pounds of brochures and other booklets. I figured I would have a few months to check them out and pursue some leads on resources for my small business. I guess God had another plan for me. Shortly after my visit to the center, Vicki called me because she wanted me to connect with the Center's director, Susan Davis. Of course, she was another dynamic woman with drive and intensity for women's success in their chosen endeavors. Shortly after meeting with Susan, I was introduced to Dr. Linda Salane. Unfortunately, the Center for Women Entrepreneurs closed a few months later. Vicki and Susan took on different roles at the college and things kept moving forward for all of us. Vicki began working closely with Dr. Salane to organize and promote various events for the college as well as women in the local community and across the state. Before long, I was involved with a summer leadership camp for girls, round table discussions for women in business, focus groups and monthly leadership forums for women. Although I can't remember what happened to all of that paper, I can talk for hours about my experiences with my Columbia College family. The people I have met, the relationships I have established, the things I have learned and the support I have received from them have been phenomenal. Words can not express my gratitude.

My journey with the family at the Leadership Institute of Columbia College has been priceless. On November 11, 2002, I was presented with a special opportunity. I was invited to the college president's house for dinner and conversation with Julie Dolan, oldest sister of the Satellite Sisters public radio show. Julie was visiting South Carolina as a part of *Satellite Sisters' Uncommon Senses* book tour. Wow! This was an opportunity to meet a woman well ahead in the game. I knew we had a lot in common. She was living abroad as a result of her husband's job. She was the glue that held her nuclear family unit together in foreign places. In addition to her vital role in the family, she was a business woman and an author. That was enough to gain my attention and attendance at the dinner. I did not want to miss this opportunity.

Although Julie was the magnet for the event, she was not the dominant force of the conversation. Dr. Linda Salane captured it best when she observed that the room was filled with so much talent from such a powerful group of dynamic women. I really appreciated her comments simply because I saw myself as a come along sister to the affair to learn as much as I could. Yet, as I reflected back on the evening, I saw it as an affair from which we learned and gained something from all of the participants' contributions to the discussion. We all had time to ask Julie questions about living abroad, the Satellite Sisters debut on the Oprah Winfrey Show and their featured column in the Oprah Magazine. Each of us shared pieces of our journey as women and the various obstacles we encountered in pursuit of our personal and pro-fessional goals. As the dinner came to an end, we were able to recognize our own satellite sisters in our lives. Even if they are not biological sisters, it's great to have a group of women to be connected to for various supporting roles in our lives.

Later that evening, Julie was able to share with us the Dolan Sisters' take on life and leadership. Fortunately, I had checked out a copy of *Uncommon Senses* from the public library to read some of her work. In a nutshell, these sisters have agreed on the five uncommon senses that are necessary for success in the big world. We must have a sense of con-nection, a sense of self, a sense of humor, a sense of adven-ture and a sense of direction. This was an incredible evening. I walked away from that event with a greater appreciation for my efforts to be a satellite sister to others. Previously, I had not thought of things packaged quite that way. I have spent some time assessing my uncommon sens-es at this stage in my life. Some of my uncommon senses are keener than others, but I can work with them.

As I reflected back on my days prior to the beginning of my writing project, I can recognize the marked improvement of my relationship to other women. I can even identify some satellite sisters. Regardless of their roles as supporter, moti-vator, sister or confronter, I know that these are direct fruits from my connection to the Leadership Institute. Although the Center for Women Entrepreneurs no longer operates, I have found an even greater niche at the Leadership Institute.

Ladies, I love you! Keep blazing those trails and paving the way for the women of South Carolina and around the world.

On Appreciation...
"Always remember to say thank you."
-Karren Hill Gordon

Chapter 11:

Special Thanks to My Brothers and Sisters

As I reflect back on days past, I cannot in good faith complete this project without saying thank you to many others that have shown countless acts of care and concern for me. These small and selfless acts made all the difference during some long days and challenging times.

I say thank you to my brothers: Brian Keith Gamble for being a true friend and a great math tutor; John Howard, Sr. for being there for me and my family; Mike Gannon for your listening ear and encouraging words; Ellis White, Jr. for all of your prayers and laughter; Vince Ford for your encouragement and suggested readings; Stephen Gilchrist for your friendship and strategy sessions; David Weeks and Steve Benjamin for sustaining my interest in politics; Patrick Bennett for helping a stranger on the side of the road; and my grandfather, the late Andrew Hill for the precious memories.

I say thank you to my sisters: Margaret Stokes for taking me under her wing at the University of South Carolina; Anna Valdez for the warm welcome to Texas; Wynette Randolph and Lavern Simmons for taking such good care of little Kristen while I worked; Nelva Davenport-Sneed for being a true friend and prayer partner; Lois Howell for your support and loyalty; Cynthia Bremeyer for the Governor's EXCEL Institute bond and friendship; Joann Moton for your support and encouragement; my aunt, Mary Pringle for the consistent check-in phone calls over the years no matter where I lived; Rev. Telley Gadson for your care and many prayers; Sandra Bryan and Becky Bailey for your support and leadership efforts; Marcia Kelly for your inspiration and example of inner strength; the Mount Zion United Methodist Women for nurturing me; my grandmother, the late Adeline Dicks, for sharing her humble spirit and compassion; and the late Patricia Watson for her confidence in my ability.

I was once told that people enter your life for a reason or a season. I thank God for all of you. I know that it was nothing special about me but something very special about you. As a result of your help and encouragement, I try everyday to be of assistance to someone else. Much has been given to me and provided for me. For that, I am very grateful.

<u>What Can I Do?</u>

1.

2.

3.

Action Steps

1.

2.

3.

My Network

Name _____
Address _____
_____
Phone _____
Email _____

Name _____
Address _____
_____
Phone _____
Email _____

Name _____
Address _____
_____
Phone _____
Email _____

Name _____
Address _____
_____
Phone _____
Email _____

Name _____
Address _____
_____
Phone _____
Email _____

Name _____
Address _____
_____
Phone _____
Email _____

Name _____
Address _____
_____
Phone _____
Email _____

Name _____
Address _____
_____
Phone _____
Email _____

Graduation at Webster University

Mom, dad, and my daughter, Kristen with
me after commencement.
Columbia, South Carolina 1999

About the Author

Karren Hill-Gordon is a native of Sumter, South Carolina. She attended the public schools in Sumter County School District 17 and graduated from Sumter High School in 1982. She earned a Bachelor of Science degree in Criminal Justice from the University of South Carolina and received a Master of Arts degree in Management from Webster University in 1998. Mrs. Hill-Gordon is a member of Phi Beta Kappa, American Association of University Women-Greater Columbia Branch, South Carolina Advocates for Women in Public Service, Mt. Zion United Methodist Church in Sumter, South Carolina and the United Methodist Women Organization. Hill-Gordon is the co-owner of Gordon Associates Management Consulting Firm and founder of the Support Your Sister (SYS) Network-Greater Columbia Area. She is married to Christopher Gordon and they have one daughter, Kristen Marie. Hill-Gordon has a special interest in empowerment opportunities, skill building/ enhancement and image consulting for young women.